DESIGN ROAD TRANSPORT HOW BRINGS

ECONOMIC BENEFIT

JOHN LOK

Contents

Preface

Preface

Nowadays, transportation and economic development have close relationship. Economic development stimulates transportation demand by increasing the numbers of workers commuting to and from work, customers traveling to and from services areas, and products being moving by lorries on the roads between products and customers.

Part one concerns to research how road transportation design network and countries' land use has close relationship. Thus, I shall concentrate on researching the relationship between offices and factories and shopping centers, schools etc. building and designing networks and land use and economic growth relationship aspect. I shall recommend methods how to design road network to solve traffic jam, air pollution, over pedestrian population walking on the street etc. challenges. The most important concerning is to research whether designing road network system can have close relationship to assist any countries' economic growth . I shall give ideas to explain this issue occurred possibly. If readers like to do research writing, I believe that this book is very suitable to them to be used for reference.

Part two concerns why MTR underground train transportation needs to know passenger behaviour. What are the factors to cause passengers who choose to catch other transportation tools? Indicating methods how to solve passenger choice challenges to attract many passengers who will choose MTR to catch more than other kind of transportation tools. It is suitable to any readers who have interest to learn how to use transportation behaviour strategy to solve passenger behavioural choice.

My aim to write this book which concerns how to design road transportation network to assist road transportation to reduce time spending to transport any products in the short time efficiently and to rise economic growth in any countries.

Prologue

Table of contents

ONE

Transport Design Advantages

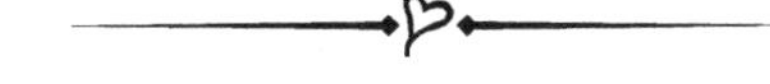

The Economic Influence Of The Crisis Of Road Traffic Fatalities In Japan

Any country need to design road transporttion system. For example, the Japan country lacks design road trsnaportation system effectively. So, the crisis of road traffic fatalities will raise and the econominc influence will be changed. The crisis indicates more than 7,000 people die annually as a result of motor vehicle crashes in Japan. Driving when under the influence of alcohol is the leading cause of motor vehicle crash fatalities in both developed and developing countries. So, alcohol is the most serious factor to raise personal risk when drivers are driving in Japan. However, a number of studies have shown that deterring drink driving is an important way to cause fatalities. There is a demonstrative need for social change in Japan.

Japan has recently strengthened its already strict laws in order to reduce the number of alcohol related road fatalities. Those deforms lowered the legal blood alochol contant limit increased, the penalties for offenders. The Japan road traffic legal needs. Any driving a motor with a alcohol limit of 0.03 or higher Japan's maximum sentence is up to 3 years imprisonment or a fine not exceeding 500,000 yen dollars. Is law impact to reduce drinking alcohol to drive in Japan? What are economic influence of the crisis of road traffic fatalities in Japan?

The rational choice theory of offending suggests that offenders are active decision makers who influence a large number of variables into decision whether or not to commit an offence. On the cost-benefit analysis, it is the punishment a possible jail, large fines worth is the reward the convenience of driving home without the expause of a taxi and innovenience to the alcohol drivers in Japan. Instead of law reforms when it detects alcohol in the air exhaled from the alcohol and other offenders and it educates children about the dangers of drinking and it also explains why alcohol driving can also threaten drivers' life when who are drinking alcohol and driving behaviour in the same time in Japan.

On the economic influence hand, implementation of the policy deregulating alcohol sales and alcohol production did not appear to increase traffic fatalities among adult or teenage males or females in Japan. We found that male adult fatalities demonstrated a statistically significant decline following enactment of the deregulation policy in 1994 year. So, Japan implement law to threaten alcohol drinking behaviour is useful. It can influence the alcohol availability and consumption, alcohol production and sales, the 24 hours operated convenience stores or liquor discount stores incomes to be reduced. Even, Japan overall GDP is also reduced from the deduction of liquor alcohol production and sale, also the occurrence of traffic accident fatalities chances will be also reduced.

The Japanese economy has entered a rapid process of liberalization since the mid-1990 year. Many sectors previously under direct government control are now regulated by the competitive market place. The Japanese alcohol beverage market has changed. The entry of cheaper import alcohol products resulted in a encouragement of alcohol consumption to Japan drinking drivers and an raising of increasing of more import alcohol products supply to Japan. Although, it is beneficial to Japan GDP growth. But it also raise the occurrence of chance to traffic accidents rate to cause alcohol drinkers to be death or hurt when who choose drinking alcohol to drive at the same time in Japan. So, alcohol import can bring more consumption, but it can also raise many traffic accidents occurrence in Japan in the same time.

In conclusion, alcohol is not good for health to drink when the consumer often buys alcohol at drink habitually. So, if many Japanese, including the alcohol driving consumers and the alcohol non drinking consumers both who often buy different countries alcohol to drink daily. It will cause their bodies to be unhealth for long term in Japan. It is possible to increase Japan's government's medical expenses to assist the low income or poor people in the future. So, although alcohol import can raise Japan GDP growth in the short term, but it also raise Japan government's medical expenditure to the low income or poor Japanese long term in the future, So it's economic benefit will not good in the future if Japan still import much alcohol to sell in its country.

Many commercial users depend on road transport facilities, with movement of products and services from place to place on the roads, aspect of global and urban economic survival. Hence, developments of various transportation modes have become important to physical and economic developments. For example, urban locations with such relative advantages are found where different transport routes with high degree of connectivity, within the intra and inter urban road networks. On similarly, commercial activities like banking, retail/wholesale businesses and professional services can take advantage of nearness to concentration of activities attracted consumers service providers. This partly caused increase in demand for commercial space and its effects on commercial property values along commercial roads can be rose. However, some countries' roads need to provide pedestrian movements more than the businesses activities, e.g. shorten the time of lorries parking on the road to let pedestrian movements on the narrow road. If the country government did not consider the roads need to let more pedestrian movements or shorten the time of lorries parking on the road. It will cause traffic jam or traffic density of the individual roads. Hence, governments need to concern the locations of commercial property buildings and the relationship between the explanatory variables of the design road networks.

What are construction of roads design networks benefits?
Nowadays, transportation and economic development have close relationship. Economic development stimulates transportation demand by increasing the numbers of workers commuting to and from work, customers traveling

to and from services areas, and products being moving by lorries on the roads between products and customers. According to Bailey, Mokhtarian and Little (2008) indicated "transportation route is past of distinct development pattern or road network and mostly described by regular street patterns as an important factor of human existence, development and civilization. The route network combined with increased road transportation investment result in changed levels of conveniently reflected through cost benefit analysis, savings in travel time, and other benefits. " These benefits are noticeable in increased catchment areas for services and facilities , shops, schools, offices, banks and leisure activities.

In fact, construction of roads increased substantially with the opening up of residential environments that also is getting much benefits from increasing demand for spaces in commercial properties. Many private companies, retail stores, commercial banks aggregate in the main roads of cities, which get advantage of opportunities afforded by locations near central of cities to attract many pedestrians concerning their businesses existence. This led to high concentration of vehicular and pedestrian movements. Specially along the access main roads in the central of cities. The main roads exhibits linkages to form networks of minor routes along which commercial properties locate. If commercial users are displaced residential users, causing sites to be at the highest and best uses with increases in the values of commercial properties. However, it seems road network development is affected by the compact nature of various routes that sometimes causes volume of traffic jam. Thus, demand for transport can't be treated solely as a derived demand road. Improved main and minor roads access an city or rural areas is a necessary (but not sufficient). Precondition for increased productivity, the UK Standing Advisory committee On Trunk Road Assessment (SACTRA, 1999) noted "various ways in which transport can affect economic growth, for example benefits include through reorganization and rationalization of production, distribution and land use: reducing labor costs by expanding catchment areas etc."

What is land use and road transport design system relationship?

Land use refers to the whole range of human activity and of the built environment, and to some aspects of the natural environment. This is a way relationship between land use and road transport. Governments need to design how to use land and how to design road transportation systems. e.g. where are built the main roads and/or where are built the minor roads are the most suitable locations in the cities or rural areas ? If the main roads is located in the not suitable locations at the centers of the cities or rural, it will case the increasing traffic volumes and levels of congestion, including air pollution, noise, ground water pollution from run-off , loss of soil functions and loss of bio-diversity to natural environment. By influencing the spatial structure of locations in the urban environment, so land use planning can help to mitigate any negative effects resulting from land use changes.

Modelling and land use transportation interactions has become an important aspect of road design transport planning. On the one side, for example, design roads in urban centers, it can increase land use and it can also reduce employees or students catching buses or driving cars' time spending to go to workplaces or schools users. Hence, the land use and roads designing transportation can give benefits to residents and employment people to reduce time to wait buses or taxies etc. public transportations to go to workplaces or schools or shopping centers etc. anywhere. It seems to assist bus companies or taxi drivers to earn more income, On the other side, designing urban transport systems is also important . Increased densities mean more destinations become within convenient walking and cycling distances and consequently the use of these modes tends to be higher. Also in dese cities public transport systems are able to offer higher levels of service and operate more economically, when the provision of sufficient road space to meet potential demand becomes impractical. It aims to reduce the danger of driving or walking in urban areas. The transport modes (that is walking, cycling, public transport) and the extent of car dependence is less, due to driving users dependency is less on rural roads. Hence, building main roads can concentrate on designing convenience to pedestrian walking to close to their houses on the streets. However, poor transport design and land use can cause to spend too expenditure not only transport costs on governments and transport users both and also the costs of providing other services. These include the usual utilities and also education and health services as well as negative externalities , such as greenhouse gas emissions. Most such studies concluded that there are significant financial and economics cost advantage of inner city redevelopment compared with fringe development.

However, such policies won't necessarily be successfully, in particular because of the two ways road problem, they may result in additional private investments and employment opportunities flowing into the region, buy may equally result in population and employment opportunities flowing out of the target region because of the improved access to other centers. Hence governments need to analyze how to arrange the land use to assist the property developers to choose where are the suitable locations to build offices or factories or shopping centers or houses at capital or urban cities to adapt to whose the growth of living population. For example, to judge where the land use whether where main roads or junior roads are built where are the suitable locations to satisfy the lorry drivers to park their lorries are the safe locations ; to design the minor roads to let the pedestrians to feel no danger to walk on the streets when the cars are driven to near to the streets on the minor roads. Thus, the factor of choosing where the land use to design the main or minor roads areas, sizes and lengths and of the minor or major roads can influence the drivers and pedestrians feel safe or dangerous when who are driving whose cars on the roads or who are walking on the streets to arrive the offices, schools, cinemas, church, houses etc. destination.

TWO

DESIGNING ROAD TRANSPORTATION NETWORKS HOW TO ASSIST ECONOMIC GROWTH

I feel it is not all transport investments will be equally effective in enhancing economic growth. Designing road transport investment is a necessary, but on its own not sufficient requirement to earn significant economic growth at either a national or regional level. There are conditions under three categories: economic conditions, investment conditions and political conditions. In fact, although in some circumstances, transport investment may be a necessary condition for enhancing economic growth, it is rarely on its own a sufficient condition. Other factors including the broader policy environment, need to be present if the investment is going to be successful in addressing regional economic objectives. My some suggestions the following key aspects as being most relevant including:

a. Scale economies for example, where these dominate, lower transportation costs through improved accessibility may encourage increased concentration of firms in core regions, until the point that diseconomies set in.
b. Size of the local market.
c. Local land and labor conditions.
d. The nature and scale of transport improvements.
e. The nature of backward and forward linkages
in the country 's local economy.

In any country, road transportation improvements don't guarantee increased economic development. To increase economic development, an improvement needs to assist any lorry drivers to drive in short trips to reduce transportation costs and shorten time driving on the road or to make transportation more reliable, e.g. reducing the numbers of traffic jams on any roads. A proper economic climate must also exist as well as other support services. With these factors to influence transportation improvements can become catalysts for economic expansion. However, road transportation improvement that intends to induce job creation, when employers need many lorry drivers to help them to transport products and to move products on the roads often. So, the employers need to employ many transportation workers and lorry drivers to help who to transport their products to send to clients, due to the transportation time is shorten and work efficiency is rasied, so the transportation times are also increasing every day when the road transportation roles are improved. On the other side, improving transportation can raise productivity when many customers need to buy many products and the lorry drivers may drive whose lorries to transport many products between factory and office or between factory to the client's home or between the shop and the client's on the road in the short time fast.

I recommend one model links in an overall road transportation network includes these four modes.

I. Maximizing use of the existing road highway system.

II. Extending or improving the multi-lane divides system local roads and connectors.

III. Continually improving the entire road highway network in response to business activities demand.

The improvement of modern road transportation successful factors include:

- How to improve the highway network

modernization includes obsolete interchanges and other segments of the road, transport network of new designs to improve the life and service of pedestrian walking streets, rebuilding certain in main or minor roads. To the extent that labor markets operate more efficiently and more jobs are created to raise economic expansion if our governments can improve road transportation system to design to satisfy business users demand when lorry drivers need to move or transport whose products on the streets, but who will not influence pedestrian are walking on the streets. Hence, excellent transportation design network can subsequent plan efforts, it can also rise economic efficiency, community and social effects, it can also encourage transportation users to attempt to drive lorries to transport products a lot of times in one day fast and who can also avoid traffic jams occurrence on the road easily. On the one side, economic development is a concept referring to the material aspects of community welfare. There are numerous factors need of development: growth in income and wealth, equitable distribution of income, decreased infant mortality rates, increased literacy rates. On the other side, economic growth means which is sustainable increase in community income and /or wealth. (wealth is the net of resources that generate income). It seems the link between transportation facilities and economic growth has close relationship. Good transportation facilities support economic growth by lowing the transportation costs of users of the transportation network, such as roads. Direct users benefits are reductions in travel, times and fuel consumption, increased reliability and increased safety in the movement of people and products, users' transportation costs are reduced, resources are used for other purpose.

- The relationship between transport and economic development occur in two directions, in the sense that (i) land use and economic development are major drivers' of demand for transport (in terms of quantity , type, location and mode); and (ii) transportation investments and other initiatives (such as regulations, pricing) can influence levels, patterns and locations of economic development. The principal role of road transportation is to provide access between spatially separated locations for the business and household sectors, for both commodity (lands transportation) and person movements. For the business sector, this involves connections businesses and their input sources between business factories and other business shops and between business and their markets. For the households sector, it provides people with access to workplaces and education facilities, shops and social recreation, community and medical facilities etc. on the roads. I feel different countries' road transportation system can be self funded in the sense that the majority of the costs of transportation system investment operation and maintenance are either paid directly by users (for example, through car operating costs) are funded initially by governments and recovered from transport users (for example, through petrol duties and road user charges). Governments' road transportation system and their use also give rise to some external costs(externalities). These include global environmental impacts (greenhouse gas emissions) and local environmental and health impacts (for example, noise partial pollution and road accident costs). The direct effects of transportation investments are to reduce road transportation time and costs through reducing travel time, decreasing the operating costs of transportation and enhancing access to destinations within the road network. A good road transportation network also needs to reduce any economic disbenefits, for example where projects reduce congestion or the risk of injury. These incremental benefits of transportation investments may be measured through commercial cost benefit analysis. Other indirect consequences of road transportation network should also be considered when evaluating effects on productivity and the spatial pattern of economic development. Good road transportation design network benefits can include lower costs and enhanced accessibility, due to better transportation links and services expand markets for individual transportation using business and improved access to input.

The economic contribution of road transportation policy can be assessed from various perspectives. These include:

- Effects on aggregate economic welfare (e.g. the sum of consumer and which is the times of cost benefit analysis, as linking to transportation productivity effect.
- Micro economic, for example, enterprise or household level productivity effects.
- Macro economics, for example, contributions to GDP investment or employment and the spatial patterns of economic activity.

One key characteristics of road transportation is split between infrastructure and operations. Infrastructure refers to the right of way on which vehicles operate, which may include ancillary facilities to ensure efficient and effective operations (for example, traffic signals, railway stations). In developed countries, are in most transportation is operated by the private cars, road trucks, the majority of bus and coach services. In long term , overall purpose, to ensure transportation system helps to develop that maximizes the economic and social benefits and minimizes harm. Hence, governments need to concern who are their main target users to use every road. Such as the road is used to near to park and leisure, or local and national economic conditions, keep clean natural environment etc. facilities to provide different benefits to different target users to enjoy to use. It seems that good transportation networks designing can influence economic activities, shopping convenience or business convenience etc. activities to cause whether the country's economic behavior to achieve close relationship successfully. Possible relationship between road networks, location attribute, demand and supply and accessibility and commercial property values of these factors which will influence different countries' concerning to choose where to build main roads and sub minor roads in different cities and rural locations. However, I shall suppose hypotheses how governments to find the most suitable places to build main roads and sub minor roads to whose cities and rural. There is no significant relationship between commercial property values and individual contributions of explanatory variables to variability in commercial property values in whose countries.

In conclusion, I suggest methods how to design suitable transportation networks to governments to build, such as it is essential to establish a technique that may be useful for determining relative accessibility of locations in the network of main roads and sub minor roads. Even, when relative advantages are determined, there is need to develop models that will be useful for predicting commercial properly values. The model may become tool for professional estate surveyors and values to change their practice of using intuition to determine relative access of locations in a road network. Similarly, there is the need to predict the supply of, demand for, and fair market values of commercial properties by developers. Hence if the cities or rural locations can attract many businesses to build commercial properties, governments can build the main roads in the locations. Otherwise, if the cities or rural locations can not attract many businesses to build commercial properties, governments can build the sub minor roads in these locations. Hence, the main roads must have high transportation valuation to let big lorries to drive and park in these main roads easily and conveniently. It seems capital cities may not influence to build the main road factors. Natural environment, commercial properties values, the lands areas size and shape and pedestrian walking numbers on the streets and lorries available numbers on the areas will be other factors to influence where to build main roads in any cities or rural in the country.

In road concept, the route network consists of primary and secondary roads, known as main roads and minor roads respectively. Main roads are usually moderate or high capacity roads that are below highway level of service, carrying large volumes of traffic between areas in urban centers and designed for traffic between neighbors. They have intersections with collector and local streets and commercial areas, such as shopping centers, petrol stations and other businesses are located along such roads. In additions, main roads link up to expressways and freeways with inter-changes in cities or rural. Road network constitutes an important element in urban development , due to urban areas have many farms, gardens, forests , so roads and building needed to provide accessibility required by different land uses and the proper functioning of such urban areas depends an efficient transport network existence. In computing des, the network indicator are used to partition road network into different parts in reasonable way. The results in number of connection to describe density differences in road networks. The parameter records how many roads connect to each road in a network. For two roads with the same length, the ones in the dense area will connect to more roads than that in a sparse area and the connection differences will indicate the density differences to some extent, so road density can also be calculated as the total length of all known roads divided by the total land area in a road divided by the total land area in a road network. Hence, governments need to consider road length to decide how to build main or minor roads to design its transportation systems for businesses activities , such as driving lorries and parking lorries and products are been moving on the streets from roads easily and conveniently. As Wikipedia Contributors (2008) indicate that "transport networks are spatial structures designed to channel flows from the points of demand to points of supply and to link the points together in a transportation system. They are useful for transport network analysis to determine the flow of people, products, services and vehicles." Hence, governments need to research whether where the shopping centers, cinemas, houses, hospitals, schools, offices, factories etc. are located, then, which need to follow these location datas to predict the cars, lorries, taxies, buses etc. of the demand numbers of transportation users to design the lengths, width and distances and the construction of main and minor roads locations and their supply numbers in different capital cities or country roads. It aims to reduce traffic jams and shorten time and air pollution as well as increasing the available spaces to let the lorry drivers to move their logistc on the road easily and reducing the accidents occurrence when the pedestrians are walking on the streets. If the vehicles can be moved on the roads easily. It will also increase time efficiency and productivity to any businessmen. Hence, how to design of the main roads and/ or minor roads in any capital or country cities. It will influence any country's economic growth long time in the future.

THREE

Underground Train Passenger Behavior

Understanding individual passenger behaviour is essential for the design MTR transportation, because who can choose to catch bus, taxi, tram, train ferry etc. different kinds of public transportation tools. Individual traveler who decides to catch which kinds of public transportation tools, it depends on whether the public transportation tool can provide real time travel information, liking link travel time schedule. So, MTR underground train needs to understand where it has terminal to give convenience to the local living areas of time travelers to choose to catch MTR easily. Although, MTR ticket fare is one factor to influence any passengers choice. But, those other factors can also influence them to choice. e.g. MTR any terminal location of convenience, short time travelling, none crowding in busy (peak) time, MTR platform waiting arrival time, none sudden MTR engineering machines broken accident events occurrence frequently etc. different factors, any one of these factors which can influence passengers who choose to catch MTR or other kinds of transportation tools.

Why route choice can influence passenger behavioural choice

Usually, the busy time passengers will regard the route choice as a coordination problem to influence them to choose to catch which kinds of transportation tools. The route choice is as an opportunity costs to influence any busy time passengers to decide to choose to catch which kind of transportation tool which is the best right choice in the right time among of them. In the short time, for example, it seems any busy time passengers will choose to catch bus to substitute MTR underground train transportation tool, due to who feels the bus can arrive any destinations to compare other kinds of transportation tools in the most short time. However even if the MTR can either charge cheaper ticket fare to sell full day or charge discount ticket fare to sell in the busy (peak) time to compare to bus fare. It is possible that the busy time passengers will still choose to catch bus, if between the bus terminal and the another bus terminal that distance is the shorter time route to spend time to arrive destination to compare between the MTR terminal to the another MTR terminal arrival time . Also, although the busy time passengers will feel to enounter traffic jam to influence sitting or waiting bus time to be longer time in possible and who also feel MTR can avoid traffic jam problem. However, usually any busy (peak) time passengers will feel the chance of traffic jam occurrence will be less. So, the short bus route choice is more potential factor to influence the busy (peak) time passengers still to choose bus to catch.

However, if anyone wants to investigate results of day-to-day route choice which can be transferred to more realistic environment. It is necessary to explore individual behaviour in an interactive experimental set up to ensure busy (peak) time passenger transportation behavioural choice. For example, a passenger has a choice between a main road (M) and a side road (S) for travelling from (A) to (B). (M) is faster if (M) and (S) are chose by the same number of passengers. So, this method can be researched whether MTR terminal station is located at the main road (M) or the side road (S) where is more suitable to accept to passengers generally.

Why trip time reliability and
crowding factors can influence
MTR passenger choice.

Other problem is MTR busy (peak) time's crowding in public transportation occurrence of MTR underground train transportation tool is becoming a growth to concern as MTR demand growth at a busy (peak) time. To capture the MTR passengers benefits with reduced crowding from improved MTR public transport service and image. It is necessary a identify the relevant dimensions of crowding that are meaningful measures of what crowding means to MTR passengers. Two main influences on MTR model choice that are growing in relevance are trip time reliability and crowding. It represents a benefit-cost framework. In fact, MTR passengers can be willing to pay more expensive ticket fare, it MTR can avoid crowding and short and the accurate arrival trip time between terminals is reliable to occur. How to measure of MTR crowding, e.g. weighting the gap between the busy time, the standard (i.e. objective) and the perceived (i.e. subjective) metrics. We are not in a position to definitely map the two dimensions, which is a crucial requirement for translating objective improvements into equivalent subjective gains that then can be applied, willingness to pay estimates MTR ticket fares to obtain the additional MTR passenger benefits of MTR public transportation investment to any terminal stations. Because MTR crowding has a negative impact on passengers in terms of psychological on emotional distress. MTR passengers are willing to stand for up to 20 minutes of the service is fast and reliable. However crowding outweighed these benefits from a MTR passenger's perpective, experienced crowding leads a increased dissatisfaction. e.g. stress and less privacy during who needs to stand up in MTR. Due to there are no enough places to supply to them to stand up in MTR. If the MTR trip time was longer time between the passenger's terminals, who will feel more dissatisfaction and it will cause who feels whether who ought need to choose to catch other transportation tools to substitute MTR next time. e.g. bus, train, tram, ferry, taxi etc. So, from an operator's perspective, the MTR service frequency or MTR size is significantly influenced by the level of ridership, which sends a signal to respond if the monitored crowding level exceeds the benchmark standard in the busy time. e.g. in the morning time or at the night time, the students or employment people who need to go to schools or offices (working places). The locations of different places between MTR terminals and crowding are regarded as a key service attribute for MTR pubic transportation along with other factors, such as travelling time and reliability, e.g. service quality, none engineering machines are broken to cause MTR stops suddenly.

Given the increasing importance of crowding on both the disutility to existing MTR public transportation users and the influence to it. MTR passenger can choose to use either the MTR public public transportation or other public transportation. It is timely to review the MTR current measures of crowding defined by transportation authorities. MTR operators ought evaluate whether they apporpriately reflect MTR each traveler experiences and perceptions of crowding in busy (peak) time. I suggest that MTR needs to buy other underground trains to supply to the busy (peak) time passengers to let them have enough seats to sit down, so who do not need to stand up in any MTR underground trains when they catch MTR underground trains in busy time. It aims to let who are willingness to pay the estimation of reasonable ticket fares to compare the other kinds of transportation tools in the busy (peak) time.

What is the crowding difference
between train and MTR underground train.
In fact, crowding won't be happened to brother these transportation tools easily in the busy time and non busy time both. e.g. bus, taxi, train, tram, ferry. Because passengers can not choose to stand up in these transportation tools easily, due to these transportation tools have no enough areas (spaces) to let them to stand up easily . So, the crowding will be avoided to occur in these tranportation tools usually. Otherwise, MTR will have many passengers who can choose to stand up because MTR design of length is very long and it has enough areas (places) to let passengers to choose to stand up, even there have none any seats are provided to let them to sit down. So, MTR passengers will feel more dissatisfaction and crowding easily, especial in any peak (busy) time every day.

Comparing to bus, much more diverse crowding measures are defined in the passenger rail industry. For passenger, different specifications for measuring crowding are found across countries and even within a country. For example, rail crowding measures in the UK, the passengers in excess of capacity is crowding measure that applies to all London and South east operators weekday train services at a London terminus during the morning peak from 0700 to 09: 59 , and those departing during the afternoon peak from 16:00 to 18:59 (office of rail regulation 2011 year). The overall PIXC figure is considered the planned standard class capacity of each train service as well as the actual number of standard class passengers on the service at the critical point. i.e. the location on a trains of standard class passengers that surpass the planned capacity as the difference between the number of actual passengers and the capacity of the train divided by the number of passenger is within the capacity . So, it seems train and MTR underground public transportaton tools had been encountering the crowding problems in peak time, the difference in train passengers need to wait next train or more train arrival is who doesn't plan to enter the train, when who discovers the current train has no seats to provide to them to sit down in whose trip. Otherwise, MTR passengers can choose either to stand up within the large areas (places) if who discovered there are no any seats to provide to them to sit down or who can wait the next MTR arrival in order to who can sit down. It seems MTR transportation tool crowding environment includes in waiting platform and inside of the MTR underground train. Otherwise, train transportation tool crowding environment only includes the waiting platform and the passengers will not have crowding feeling inside of the train, due to none of passengers choose to stand up inside any trains because any train inside has no enough places to let them to stand up.

How MTR can attract many passengers.

On the commuter departure time choice of any reference point researching hand, the departure time decisions of communters are of fundamental importance of peak period MTR traffic congestion. However, whether on the demand side, MTR underground train congestion relief measures, such as MTR ticket fare to every terminal station needs to be charged cheaper fare or discount fare in the peak (busy) time every day. To aim to attract many passengers to choose to catch MTR Underground train public transportation tools, substitute to choose other public transportation tools in the peak time.

Over the past decades, there have been very active research efforts in the departure time problem, both in econometric modeling and dynamic user equilibrium fields. Although, these works provide valuable insights into dynamic commuter decision making, they do not identify the commuters' response to gains and losses related to whole actual arrival time to reference points who may have relative. The appliability of the reference point hypothesis of prospect theory to the commuter's departure time decision making to obtain a better understanding of how departure time choice in MTR platform during their waiting underground train arrival time. However, every MTR underground train actual arrival time and deviation variables related to reference points (gains and losses) are the key factors in the departure time choice model. How the MTR underground train of every communter's daily departure time decision can be modelled when the reference point hypothesis of prospect theory. The MTR underground train's schedule delay is defined as the difference between the preferred arrival time (PAT) and the actual arrival time (AT) for a given MTR communter. In a daily MTR commute, a commuter in the indifference band actual arrival time is an essential feature of MTR schedule study. Two reference points are the earliest acceptable arrival time and the work starting time for a given MTR platform waiting passengers. In psychological view point, prospect theory proposes that the displeasure of a loss is perceived or greater than the pleasure of a gain of the same attitude and therefore, the value function is stronger for losses than gains.

To conclude, it seems that if MTR waiting passengers need not spend long time to wait underground train arrival in platform and it can provide seats to let them to sit down in the busy (peak) crowding time. It will make them to feel pleasure, even the MTR ticket fare is not fair and reasonable to charge higher fare to compare other kinds of public transportation tools fares. So the peak waiting time factor can influence the passengers to choose other kind of transportation tools to catch easily. Moreover, MTR's two reference points are the earliest role. Similarly a loss is observed when the MTR platform waiting commuter experiences or actual arrival time which is beyond that the MTR schedule time. Due to that a MTR waiting commuter is as an early side arrival of whose actual arrival time is earlier than whose preferred arrival time.

Reference

Bailey, L., Mokhtarian, P.L. Little, A. (2008). The broader Connection Between Public Transportation, Energy Conservation And Greenhouse Gas Reduction, Report Prepared As Part Of TCRP Project J-11/Tasks Transit Cooperative Research Program, Transportation Research Board Submitted To American Public Transportation Association in http://www.apta.com/research/into/online/

land_use.cfmi, accessed 17 April 2008.

The UK Standing Advisory Committee On Trunk Road Assessment (SACTRA) (1999). Transport And The Economy (Report To UK DETR). Retrieved From: http://webarchive.nationalarchives.gov.uk/ 20050301192906 ; http://dft.gov.uk/stellent/groups/dft-econappr/documents/pdf/dft_econappr_pdf_022512.pdf

Wikipedia Contributors (2008). Arterial Roads In Wikipedia, The Free Encyclopeda, http://en.wikipedia.org/ w/ index.php?title=Arterial_road&oldid=212832640(accessed May30,2008).

9 798887 496740

Printed by Libri Plureos GmbH in Hamburg,
Germany